Here is a devotional that will inspire, uplift and empower you every day. Whatever you're facing, *A Dose of Encouragement* helps you to realize that God is in the middle of every circumstance. It will help you to handle life's challenges and walk more confidently in your Kingdom assignment.

Presented to:
_____

By:
_____

Date:
_____

Occasion:
_____

A Dose Of Encouragement

40 Days
To Inspire, Uplift and Empower You!

Sarah Branch

Dante's Publishing • Atlanta, Georgia

Copyright © 2011 by Sarah Branch. All rights reserved

Unless otherwise indicated, all Scripture quotations are taken from the King James, Message or Amplified version of the Bible.

No portion of this publication may be duplicated, stored or transmitted in any form (electronically, photocopies, recordings, scanning, storage....) without written permission of the copyright holder, except as provided by United States Copyright Law.

Library of Congress Control Number:

ISBN: 978-0-9838687-1-2

For Information or additional copies of this book, contact

Minister Sarah Branch

(202) 352-6006

Cover and Interior Design by Badie Designs

Dedication

I dedicate my book in loving memory to my grandparents: Enquin and Sarah Saxton and Lendora Branch. And to my loving Aunt Martha Helen.

This book has been long awaited. The Lord inspired me each morning to write a word of encouragement to those who need it. When He said to call it *A Daily Dose of Encouragement*, I never thought that the Spirit of God would give me a daily word. Each morning when I woke up to meet Him, He was so gracious and met me. This season has been such an important one for me because this is the closest that I have been in relationship with God. For years I thought that I had it going on and was in good standing with the Lord but I discovered that I was being deceived. Little did I know that my status with Him was in trouble. I asked the Father to do whatever He needed to do within me. God showed me the real me! Did I like what I saw? Of course not, but it was at this point that I knew that He loved me enough to allow me to get it right. Today, I can say that my relationship with Him has grown and I owe Him everything. I have discovered that success is not defined by the amount of money you have, or how many material possessions you have accumulated. Success for me is to be smack dab in the middle of God's Will for my life. When I am in His Will, I have complete peace, walk in total obedience to Him and find that trusting the Lord is not an issue. So as you take this 40-day journey with me, I pray that you can feel the very presence of God and that you will be inspired, uplifted and empowered for each day. To God be the glory for a dream coming true in my life!

Acknowledgements

I would like to acknowledge and express gratitude for the following people who impacted my life. I will never forget all that you have done for me and I appreciate all of you.

I thank my Lord and Savior Jesus Christ, who along with the Father and the Holy Spirit kept me and I will be forever grateful.

My parents: William Earl and Barbara Lorraine Saxton Branch, you mean everything to me. Thank you for displaying your strength, faith, love and never giving up on me. You've been my #1 supporters and I will always love you for that. When I didn't think that I could or didn't want to, you were always there to encourage me and you don't know what that did for me to know that I could depend on you no matter what.

My three kids: Jasmine, Donté and Ebony Branch. I love you guys so much. Thanks for sharing your mommy with so many others that needed me.

My brothers: Dexter and Derrick Branch and Eugene Henry; sisters: LaToya Bellamy and Angela Branch; cousins: Enquin (Enquincia) Saxton, Corey (Ashley) Tyson and Chris (NéTaushe) Williams; My sister (cousin) Renee (Dimitrio, Isaiah and Emmitt) Cox. What can I say other than you are the best.

My grandfather: James Branch, Sr.

My aunties: Ella Saxton (Curtis), Sarah Tyson and Deborah (Diamond) Gore for always being there.

My other grandmothers: Lucy Arrendell (MaMa Lucy), Ida Keys, Georgia Herron, Alice Hawkins and Naomi Wilson and their families.

My Destiny Pushers: Pastor Linda Caldwell, Rev. Lynda Brown-Hall, Prophetess Rosalind (Phillips) Kimbrough, Pastor Fabian Q. Tucker (Jacqueline), Rev. Ann Vessels, Pastor Tommy (Beverly) Terrell, Apostle

Margo M. Valentine, Prophet Gregory and DeeDee Bradley, Dr. Karen (Steve) McPherson, Elder Nathaniel Akers (Maria Henderson), Patrice Lancaster and Shimeka Dukes. Thank you all so much for seeing what God had in me and pushing me to my destiny, even when I didn't want you to. You kept right on and I will forever be grateful to you all.

To my entire Third Baptist Church Family (Pastor, Rev. Dr. Michael and Janet Hopkins); Godparents, Pastor Donald and Lady Liz Anderson (Bethel Church of Salvation, Capitol Heights, MD); My Bishop forever, Bishop Kevin (Denise) Gresham (entire Greater St. John Church Family, Upper Marlboro, MD), who always kept it real in my life; Pastor Stanley (Mamie) Byrd (Harvest International Church, Raleigh, NC), thank you for recognizing the calling on my life; Rev. Dr. John(Lady Karen) Franklin (Morning Star Missionary Baptist Church Family, DC); Rev. John and Kathy Waymmann (John John and Karla); Rev. Ola "Mat" Cooper; Nathaniel (Boss) and Gladys Ward; Joyce Brown, My Cheetah family: Rev. Viola Anthony, Sherita Miles and Angela Smith and I can't forget Auntie Rev. Ruth Whitehead and the newest addition, Kathleen Jones.

And to all who gave me a word of encouragement, spoke life, prayed for me and believed in me and who is a source of inspiration for this book. I love you!

Table of Contents

Dedications

Acknowledgements

Day 1 - It's Time To Get Up!... 1

Day 2 - What Are You Waiting On …Tomorrow?....................................... 2

Day 3 - Not Another Excuse.. 3

Day 4 - Discouraged But Determined 4

Day 5 - Your Life Depends On This One 6

Day 6 - "You've Been Around This Mountain Too Long!" 8

Day 7 - "On The Other Side Of Go!" 10

Day 8 - When God Interrupts Your Comfort Zone 11

Day 9 - Spoiled Brat Mentality! 13

Day 10 - Get Out Of The Way 15

Day 11 - I've Made Up My Mind... 16

Day 12 - Walking On "God Can Do Anything Street" 17

Day 13 - I'm Glad You Think It's Impossible 19

Day 14 - Don't Go Back.. 20

Day 15 - Watch Out! 21

Day 16 - Don't Let The Enemy Catch You Loafing................................. 22

Day 17 - There Is No Place Like Being In God's Presence.................... 24

Day 18 - Now What?... 25

Day 19 - "Don't Count Me Out!" 27

Day 20 - It Ain't Over Yet!... 29

Day 21 - "I Know It's Going To Be Alright" 30

Day 22 - Take Off Those Glasses.. 31

Day 23 - I Sent The Holy Ghost To Break Up This Party....... 33

Day 24 - On The Wings Of Waiting 34

Day 25 - There Is Power Behind What We Say...................... 36

Day 26 - Stop "Trippin"... 38

Day 27 - Your Thinking Is Too Small 40

Day 28 - Stay In Your Lane 42

Day 29 - Everybody Can't Go 43

Day 30 - Help Me, I'm Being Held Hostage By Unforgiveness 44

Day 31 - I'm Finally Walking Out Of This Prison.................... 46

Day 32 - Passing The Test Of Obedience................................ 48

Day 33 - If It Ain't Broke Don't Fix It 50

Day 34 - Caller Are You There? 52

Day 35 - Celebrate Your "Elevators" 54

Day 36 - There's Something Great In You and It's Time
That You Stir It Up.. 56

Day 37 - You Were Not Called To Do Pigeon Ministry......... 58

Day 38 - You Messed With The Wrong One This Time! 60

Day 39 - There Is Power In Your Praise! 62

Day 40 - Unstoppable 63

About The Author

Day 1 – "It's Time To Get Up!"

As I laid in bed one particular morning the Word of the Lord came to me saying "Get Up!" You have been playing hide and seek too long. You have just been 'laying in the cut' hoping and praying that I would just leave you alone, but there is too much in you for Me to keep allowing you to do nothing. Don't you know who you are? Don't you know that I have a lot at stake in you? Don't you know that there are people that I have assigned to you that are waiting for you? You have the nerve to just sit around and do nothing? Get Up! It's time for you to move forward. It's time for you to get your creative juices flowing. I've already put it in you and you only need to stir it up. I hear you..."you don't feel like it," I kept thinking. "I don't want to be hurt again. I've been there and done that and to go and do that again, Lord why are you playing? God, I'll be back in the game in a little bit" I argued. God said to me, "I will not say it again; it's time for you to get up. I've allowed you to do you and said nothing. I've allowed you to help everybody else. I've allowed you to do other things that were really busy--nothing that I had planned for you. I told you what I was going to do with you. I had a talk with you and showed you the promises that I have for you. I've even given you a snap shot of what's to come and you're still having a problem with moving? OK, then you have left me no other choice than to show you." As I received the warning from God I knew within myself that this time He was not playing with me. Because of His love for me and His desire for my best life, chastening would soon follow. The Bible says that God chastens those whom He loves. I know that it's only to reassure us that He knows what's best for us. He doesn't want us to just do nothing. He knows that the enemy lies waiting to steal the time by distracting us with minor things, just to get us off focus. So God intervenes and says "Hello, My Child, it's time. Get Up! Let's Go! Time has been ticking away!" So I just want to inspire you today to get Up and do what God has called you to do. It's in you. So why are you waiting on tomorrow?

Reflections:
Make up your mind, it's time to get up and do what God told you to do!

Day 2 - What Are You Waiting On... Tomorrow?

One of the famous Gospel songs back in the early 90's was called "Tomorrow" by the Winans. "...tomorrow, I'll give my life, tomorrow, I thought about today but it's so much easier to say. Tomorrow, who promised you tomorrow...for tomorrow very well might be too late."

Oftentimes we put off to another day that which we think can be done tomorrow. What I have dealt with in my own life is that tomorrow never comes due to my procrastination. There are many people who die and never finish what they needed to do because they kept putting it off. They honestly believed that they had a lot of time to do it. Tomorrow never arrives, for many people, because they end up putting something off day after day.

As much as I would like to tell you that I always get things done and never put them off, to say so would be the farthest from truth. I have had to deal with the spirit of procrastination. <u>Procrastination habitually puts off doing things and always saying that it can be done later. Many times, "later" never comes</u>. The sad thing is that everyone, at one time or another, procrastinates. It's not always our intent; however, we sometimes have too many other things that we try to make happen.

Edward Young said "Procrastination is the thief of time." We waste time when we keep putting off what we know we should do.

So what are you waiting for? Are you hoping for it to just drop in your lap? More times than not, it will not happen that way. You have to just make up in your mind that you are not going to put that activity aside any longer and just do it. Make up in your mind that you will get it done. No more excuses!

Reflections:
Do you keep on putting off things? It's not good for you. When you have to cram and do it at the last minute you sometimes miss out on other things.

Day 3 - Not Another Excuse

Isn't it amazing that we can come up with excuses when we don't want to do something? We make up an excuse when we are late; we make an excuse when we can't complete an assignment; or should I just say that we just make excuse for anything that we honestly don't like or want to do. It's one thing to know how to do something but another thing to make up in our minds that we don't want to do it just because we do not want to deal with some stuff.

Have you ever just thought about why you keep doing this? There is something more than what's seen on the surface as the reason you keep making excuses. Since we generally make excuses for things that we don't want to do, I ask you, have you ever stopped and asked yourself, why is it that you don't want to do what you know you should be doing? What are you afraid of? What's holding you back? Will this mean that you will have to stop doing some things that you may not want to stop doing? Will you have to make a change? Will you have to do something that you've never done before? Did you ever think that maybe you need to be doing some things differently? Maybe this is the one thing that God has been waiting for, just to see what you will do this time? Go and do what you've got to do.

Francais de la Rochefaucauld said: "We have more ability than will power and it is often an excuse to ourselves that we imagine things are impossible." <u>An excuse is a crutch that we like to grab hold to and hide behind</u>. We can sit back and waste time making up an excuse why we can't do or we can just do it. So the next time you want to make an excuse, counteract your excuse with determination and deal with the real reason that you don't want to do what you're dealing with. It easy to make an excuse but it's a challenge to actually do it.

Reflections:
What excuses have you allowed to stop or interrupt you from doing what God has called you to do?

Day 4 - Discouraged But Determined

In life we find ourselves in a state of discouragement. Discouragement is a tool that the enemy will use to keep us from having hope and trusting in God. At one time or another, we all have become discouraged. We have gone down the "I Don't Care Blvd." and have dealt with "I Feel Like Giving Up Syndrome."

It's not that we find ourselves discouraged but it's the fact that we can't remain in that state. We look for other people to come and rescue us. In fact when we look for someone to help us that's when we find out that no one comes along. We help everyone else but when discouragement hits our house, no one seems to want to come over. That's why the Bible tells us that David had to sometimes encourage himself. Sometimes I have to tell myself to get up you can't stay there. I have to tell myself that I can do it; that I will make it; that trouble won't last always; that joy is coming; that peace is here; that no matter what it looks like God is in control. If God allowed it, I must be able to handle it. So self, take courage in the Lord for He is your strength. When I get a little weary I know that I can just stop and look back over my life and realize that God has been too good to me to stay in that place, so then I begin to become even more determined. Determined that I am going to hold on! Determined that I can make it! Determined that it's going to be alright! Determined that even though I've been pressed and surrounded on every side; troubled and oppressed in every way; that God didn't allow it to crush me. Even though I may have suffered embarrassments and are not sure of what to do at times and sometimes unable to find a way out; I was not driven to throw in the towel because I can trust that God knows what to do. I may have been thrown down to the ground, but I was never broken or destroyed.

<u>I stand on the fact that God has never left me and His word tells me that He will never leave me</u>. So on today, even though you may be discouraged, disappointed, and want to throw in the towel, know that

trouble doesn't last always; trials come but they are only temporary. Hold on, don't let go. Trust in God; believe that He has your best interest at heart. He knows what you are going through. It's all good. You are stronger than you think!

Reflections:
Today I am determined that I will:

Day 5 - Your Life Depends On This One

There are times in our lives that we must face the fact that we will one day have to make life changing decisions. Decisions that depend on whether you live or not, whether you have victory or you are defeated, whether you sink or swim, if you will be successful or not or whether you will stay stuck in your situation or become free. This could be the very decision that could allow us to be in the will of God or just going around the same mountain yet again. This decision that you make could be the one that will determine if you will follow Christ or continue in your sinful ways. When our life depends on the decisions that we make, we have to be careful who we consult for advice.

Sometimes making a decision can be overwhelming and hard. That's why it's important that before you even decide on an issue, you need to first seek God. <u>Nine times out of ten, we make decisions based on the wrong things</u>. We base them on other people's opinions. We base them on how we feel, which way our emotions are going, we base them on what we see at the moment, or what others think is right for us. But the sad part about it is that others don't know what you need and their decision for you could end up messing you up and everyone attached to your decision. That why I love David so much, because the Bible tells us that he knew just what to do. He sought the Lord. When it came down to him making a life-changing decision, he asked God, should I pursue after the people who raided our town. Should I overtake them? God told him yes, pursue, overtake and He added a bonus you will recover all, everything…. His life as well as God's people depended on this one. The Bible also tells us in Revelation 1:8, "I Am Alpha and Omega, the beginning and the end." If God already knew what I would be from the beginning and He knows what the end of my life would be, then why would I consult someone other than Him? The enemy will have you all over the place with your emotions, feelings and flesh wanting and hoping that you would make the wrong decision. But if you seek God first you can never go the wrong way or make the wrong decision. Sometimes the decisions have the appearance to us and others as being the wrong one, but trust in the fact that God only wants what's best for us and leading us in the wrong path is not in His makeup.

Reflections:
Whatever choices you have to make, seek God for the right answer. Your life and your destiny depends on it.

Day 6 - "You've Been Around This Mountain Too Long!"

Have you ever found yourself back at the same place that you said you were never going to visit again? If you said it once you said it 100 times but somehow you find yourself right back in the exact place you said that you would never be. It's as though you were running in place or even going around the block over and over again. In your mind you thought you were actually going somewhere just because you were moving. You thought you were going forward but actually you had only been circling the same mountain yet again.

In our lives, we sometimes repeat the same vicious cycle. Sometimes we are not even aware that we keep doing the same thing because we've done it for so long. We think that since we are still alive; we are okay and that this is the way that it's suppose to be. We keep doing the same thing and expecting different results. In Deuteronomy 2:2-3, God told Moses, "you have circled this mountain long enough, it's time to turn." In other words it's time to do something different than what you've been doing. You are about to take a different route but don't be scared, God says "I got you and I will actually make them afraid of you." Because you have not been this way before, because your mind will try and play tricks on you and make you think that you are scared because this is something new, let me tell you, don't be scared. The enemy wants you to be scared because this is new territory and you've never done this before because I need to get you to where you need to go in your journey. <u>You've allowed distractions to delay you long enough</u>; I've got to move you forward."

Some of us have been circling in the same situation for days, and the days have added up to months and the months have become years. But I've come to encourage you and let you know that you have been around this mountain long enough. God wants and needs for you to move along in your journey to your destiny. You have been scared for too long, doubted too long, been stuck too long and today is the day to move forward! You need to put that dead situation to rest, and remove yourself from people in your life that leech on to you, slow you up, and keep you from moving forward.

Today begin to trust God's direction. Today begin and purpose in your heart, "I'm not going there anymore. If I go there again, this time it just might kill me, it could be the last time; this trip may just be the very one that I don't get all the way around and get to come back." In my life, I have circled the same mountain many times, but I have said in my mind, "I will not, I cannot do the same thing and expect different results. This time I've got to press forward. This time when God takes me to the Red Sea and I trust Him enough to step out onto the dry land, I can't go back to Egypt. It was a comfortable place; it was a familiar place but no longer will I pitch my tent here. It's time to journey to the promised place where God is leading me! I'm excited about where God will take me!"

Reflections:
What mountain have you circled over and over again? Ask God to give you direction and order your steps so that you can learn what you need to learn and be able to move forward.

Day 7 – "On The Other Side Of Go!"

Have you ever felt like you were supposed to be going somewhere, or that God told you that it was time to go but you found yourself unable to take steps forward? Could it be due to your fear of what's on the other side of "Go," we get stuck? We want to move and we know that we should take the steps but we allow the enemy to talk us out of going.

I can tell you from experience, how I began to tell myself, how was I actually going to get moving. What was I going to be doing when I got there? When was I supposed to start moving? What would I face when I finally got to the other side of Go! All these thoughts plus many others begin to bog my thought process and <u>going to the other side begins to look like a giant</u>.

> In Genesis 12:1, God tells Abram, "Get up and go to the place where I will show you." The interesting part is that God never gave Abram blue prints, never told him to go on MapQuest to get directions, never gave him an address to plug into his GPS tracker so that he will know turn-by-turn instructions, all He said was Go! God is telling some of us to Go! No! You will not know where you are going, how you will get there or even what's on the other side of Go! All I want for you to do is trust me and Go!

Can I just encourage you, that taking the first step in movement to the other side of "Go" is not always easy or comfortable. When you make an honest decision that you will trust God and go, I guarantee you that He will be right there waiting for you. So see what's on the other side of "Go!"

I'm so excited and can't wait to hear your stories and praise report on what happened when you started the process or even reached the other side of "Go!" What a sense of peace and freedom you will possess.

Reflections:
I don't know where I am going, but today, God I promise that I am going to go where you send me.

Day 8 - When God Interrupts Your Comfort Zone

There are times that God will be left with no other choice but to pull you out of the place where you are so that you won't miss Him again. These are the times when you are comfortable; you are content, happy, satisfied, and relaxed. In other words, you are okay right where you are; so it seems. But in actuality, some of us are not; we just don't know how to get out of where we have hung our hats. We are in between doing what God says and actually walking in what God is saying. God will allow us only so much time to get moving. When He sees that we are not doing what He has told us to do, we leave Him with no choice but to interrupt our comfort zone.

It's not that you want to be disobedient, not that you don't trust Him, but you are stuck. So when you become stuck and don't know what to do, God has to do what He has to do to get you back on your journey once again. I have had Him to disrupt my life in such a way that I probably wouldn't have moved by any other means. It hurt, I thought I would never recover; I couldn't show my face for a while, I just didn't like it. I pouted, I cried, I was determined I wasn't going to do anything. After I came back to myself and accepted truth, I tried to figure out how in the world I got there. Did it take all He allowed me to endure? Yes, but for you it may not. <u>God is willing to do all this and more. He will, even go as far as to make you mad at Him to get you where you need to be</u>. God needs you in a certain place; He has another assignment for you but you can't move on while you are in your comfort zone. In other words you have extended your stay. While you may look at it as being dragged out or even evicted, it's for your own good, it's for your next level of anointing, next level of experience, your ministry, and it's for God to be able to use you. As harsh as we may think that it is or even not fully understand, however, what will come forth when you come out of your comfort zone will literally blow your mind. You can't imagine all that God has for you. You've got to get there but you can't, being in your comfort zone. You can't get there standing still doing nothing. So when God starts to pull you out of your comfort zone, it's for your own good because He cares for you and only has your best interest at heart.

Reflections
What are you allowing to keep you stuck in your comfort zone?

Day 9 - Spoiled Brat Mentality!

How many times do we find ourselves "butting in" where we really are not supposed to be? We try to figure things out ourselves. We want things to go the way that we want them to go; we just "plain ole" want what we want and that's the final decision and choice. With this messed up mentality we find ourselves acting just like spoiled brats. You know how they can be, if they don't get what they want they act out until either they get what they want or the parent has to intervene because they have had enough.

It's time that you, yes you, understand and realize that you need to remove yourself from the equation. That means that it's no longer you in charge but God. It's no longer your way but God's way. When our spirit retreats to acting like spoiled brats, we have the nerve to want God to do what we want Him to do. How dare you just act like that! In this day and time, instead of telling God what we want, we need to ask God what does He want us to do; it's a personal thing. When we remove ourselves from the equation, we tell God, "I surrender my all to You. My life is in Your Hands. It's no longer I but it's You Lord. Lord, I'm available to You, whatever Your desire, whatever Your Will, that's what I'll do." When you remove yourself from the equation, you have on a blindfold and you allow God to do the leading and you do the trusting. We give up our rights, give up our thoughts, give up what we want to do, where we want to go and say God I surrender my all to you. God then says "Okay, I got you..." God says, "Do you really trust Me?, then let me guide you, be your light, direct your path and order your steps." It's when you have fully given yourself to the Will of God that you can remove yourself from the equation. You can trust God even the more, your faith will go even higher, the doors will unlock and access will be granted. It's only when you move out of the way and stop acting like a spoiled brat that God can do what needs to be done!

Today, rest in the power and anointing of God. Today, <u>it's time to graduate from the spoiled-brat mentality</u> and move to more grown up stuff. How can you deal with the grown up stuff if you are still trying to deal with the "foot stuff?" Put away the childish spoiled-brat mentality and take on the mind of Jesus Christ. Would Jesus act like that? I don't think so…. Since we know that He won't then why do you think you can? Humm… inquiring minds want to know. Honestly, He doesn't need your help; He just needs you to believe, submit and obey.

Reflections:
Let's be honest, how many times have you taken on this mentality? I have had to repent too many times! Lord, when I want to act like this, please send me a reminder that this is not the way that You want me to act.

Day 10 - Get Out Of The Way

One day God allowed me to see that it was me that was holding myself back. As much as I wanted to blame someone else for what has happened to me in the past, I had to realize that the person that was in the way was ME! This was a hard pill for me to swallow but it was truth. I had a problem with always wanting to be in charge. My infinite mind believed that if I were in charge then I could control my life. After a while of allowing me to think this way, God intervened and let me know that I was messing up everything. I had delayed areas in my life where I felt I should have been further along. It was as if I found myself standing still and going nowhere all because I would not get out of the way.

It was not until I was given truth, that my eyes were opened and I could no longer hide behind things I was holding on to. I could no longer blame others, I had to take full responsibility and realize "Get Out Of God's Way." <u>God was trying to take me somewhere, get me to the place in Him that I was in dire need of but it was me that would not relinquish myself to Him</u>.

Can I just encourage you on today; Get out of God's Way.... Allow Him to be Lord over your life. Allow Him to have total control of your life. Is it easy? Not at all, especially if you are like I was and wanted things to go my way. God, in His loving and kind way let me know He had my back. "I won't let you fall. People have let you down but I won't. People may have left you but I won't. People may have rejected you but I won't because I love you. I created you. I already predestined your future and know what's best for you, so let me have control. You've done it your way for some time now. Allow me have control of your life." Get out of the way! Just let go and let God!

Reflections:
Move!

Day 11 - I've Made Up My Mind

I've made up my mind that I'm going to trust God. Many times we say that we trust Him because we've heard someone else say it. It is perceived that we are super spiritual but are we? Then God allows a situation to occur just to see whether <u>it is just lip service or you made up your mind that you're really going to trust Him</u>.

To say that you trust Him is one thing, but when you really find yourself in a messed-up situation and you have no other choice, all of your options are gone, and then you want to trust Him. Not because He was your first choice but because you don't have any other choice. We should not be seeking God only after all other options have failed. God should be the first whom we seek. I know that it's hard, been there and done that and have t-shirts, key chains, hats and buttons to prove it.

I've made up my mind that when I find myself not knowing what to do, I'm going to trust God to show me, direct me and order my steps. It isn't easy to get to this place particularly if you have been hurt by many people. I've come to realize that I may not have been hurt if I would have gone to God first. So, I've made up my mind, that every decision, every situation, every promise that has not manifested, every disappointment that happens, I'm learning to trust in God. If the God that I proclaim to love and believe that can do anything but fail, then I should make up my mind to trust Him in every situation I have to face in my life.

Reflections:
Can I encourage you and let you know that He can handle it? If He couldn't He would have never said "Cast your cares on Me because I care for you. My yoke is easy and my burden is light."

Day 12 - Walking On "God Can Do Anything Street"

When my faith was being tested and there was what seemed to be no letting up, one thing after another rising in my life, my faith invited me to walk down "God Can Do Anything Street."

This was a period in my life that my faith didn't even seem to be hitting the Richter Scale. My level of faith was so low that there were moments that I couldn't get past the first day of believing what God had promised He would do. All that played in my mind was what if it doesn't happen? How will I get this done with no money? This will never happen... This has never happened before.... It would be the negative thoughts that I allowed uppermost in my mind that other people had dropped in my spirit. My mind would be locked-up and the key guarded by fear. God let me know that my faith was being held up by fear. Fear crippled me in such a way that every time I wanted to believe God and voiced that I believed Him that was as far as it got, lip service. I would be so excited by what God had told me but I would not be able to wrap my mind around the fact that God could really do anything at that particular moment. God had shown me many times before that He could do anything. However, as soon as another situation would arise, it would seem to be harder to bear than the previous one. I would somehow make a quick U-turn. There were times when I would not even get to "God Can Do Anything Street," it seemed like it was just a mere thought. I would make up in mind but there would be something that would hinder me. When I realized that I didn't make it there, I chalked it up. It began to be easy to say "Oh well, maybe next time."

God always intended for us to walk down "He Can Do Anything Street." In every situation in your life, He wants you to believe that He can. Even if what you want doesn't happen, God is still able! <u>Even if it doesn't happen right away, there's nothing etched in stone that says it won't</u>. Sometimes God is just preparing us for the coming attractions.... If He would allow some things to happen right away, some of us would just go back and not realize that it was God. Some of us just run to God when we want something and then when we get it, we forget all about God until the next time something happens. God wants to stretch our faith so that in every situation in our lives, we can run to "God Can Do Anything Street." God wants to move our level of faith from "not again" or "I thought I passed this test" to "bring it on, God got this one too." This just doesn't happen overnight but God will allow periods of testing so that you will be ready for every level of graduation in your faith.

Reflections:
Every graduation gets harder but God always prepares you. So let me just invite your faith to walk me down "God Can Do Anything Street."

Day 13 – I'm Glad You Think It's Impossible

I have had circumstances in my life where I allowed the enemy to make me believe that I was in an impossible situation. Thinking ignites your emotions to begin to move off of your thought patterns and you begin to feel a certain way based on this one thought that has now presented itself to you. The one thought now brings on the rush of many other thoughts and you find yourself in a place where you begin to doubt God. You begin to say to yourself, maybe this is too much for God to handle. Then you begin to conjure up ways that you can begin to handle things or even try to fix them. Your mind is latching on to "What if this doesn't work out?" or "Is God going to come through for me?" While everything that's in you reveals that the Holy Spirit is trying to present itself and come back to overthrow this messed up thought process to remind you what God has spoken in your life.

Then here comes a *dose of encouragement* that somehow finds its way to your memory band and says to you: <u>Don't you know that all things are possible through Christ Jesus</u>? I just needed to remind you of this one thing: Remember what the Lord has already done for you. Remember how He has already brought you through some rough situations that you thought you were not going to make it through, then you can put your thoughts on notice. When I think of the goodness of Jesus and all that He has done for me, my soul has no other choice but to praise Him and say "Thank you Jesus."

Stop thinking it's impossible, stop doubting what God can do and start thanking and praising Him. For what man thinks is impossible…it is possible with God.

Reflections:
Do you believe that God can do anything or is it just lip service?

Day 14 - Don't Go Back

Many times when we have gone through a rough time in our lives and we are trying to make a decision to go forward, time and again we end up going back to what is familiar to us. It's familiar because we've been there and done that, and we can even do it with our eyes closed. We go back because it's a safe, comfortable place. It doesn't challenge us to move or go anywhere or do anything different. When it's familiar, we don't really have to change; we don't have to make any real decisions. I tell you there will come a time when you will not be able to go back! There will come a time when God will not allow you to go back because <u>going back can prevent you from going forward</u>; going back can prevent you from going to the place where God is trying to take you and even away from your destiny. Just ask Lot's wife (Genesis 19:26), she wanted to go back. I believe that she remembered what it was like and desired to be back in the place God was telling them to leave. What was so important that she needed to go back? It's easy for you to judge if you have never desired to be somewhere that really was not where you needed to be. Yes, at times we want what we want but that doesn't mean that what we want is what's best for us. We have to understand that when God needs us to move from one place to another, He has a plan in mind. You may not know what it is, you may not want to go but if you trust that God wants what's best for you, you must trust Him enough to go. Is it easy? NO! Will you always want to go? NO! Will you have to completely trust God? YES! But in the end if you go and not look back, one day you will look over your life and say I'm sure glad that I chose to go and do what God said instead of being disobedient. It's the not knowing that keeps most of us from going. It's the not knowing and letting go of controlling our lives that hinders us. Let me encourage you, don't look back when God tells you to go, it will be well worth the journey.

Reflections:
What makes you want to go back to what you were in? What do you think you need to do in order not to desire to go back?

Day 15 - Watch Out!

When I was growing up, my mother taught me to always pay attention and be aware of my surroundings. 1 Peter 5:8 tells us "To be sober, observant, cautious, on alert at all times because the enemy is out to see who is napping, who he can catch off guard and not on their jobs." Whether you want to believe this or not, the enemy is coming after you at any cause to try and hinder, stop, detour what God has given, equipped, anointed and ordained you to do. Occasionally, we look for the enemy to come a certain way with certain people but to the enemy, it doesn't matter whom he uses at the time to try and thwart the plans that God has for your life. Many people chalk it up and say, "Oh that's life" and yes that may be the case, but don't think for one moment that the enemy does not have you on his hit list. You now have a target on your back that tells the enemy and his imps to stop at nothing to take you out. So he sends his imps out: discouragement, loneliness, frustration, anger, unforgiveness, and malice. Individually, these are bad enough but when you allow one to ride, they want to bring along all their friends. You're wondering how in the world loneliness came in when you were only frustrated?

So when you find yourself at this place, put on the garment of praise. When you begin to praise God, your situation has to change, your atmosphere changes, you spirit begins to calm down and focuses on God. I guarantee you that you will invoke the presence of God Almighty into your situation and He will meet you right where you are. He will give you a peace that will surpass all understanding. You will know this because you will have peace.

I want to encourage you to Watch Out! <u>Just when you think that life is going well, the enemy will try and sneak in to disrupt it</u>. Watch out!

Reflections:
Be vigilant, sober and on your toes. The enemy would like nothing more than to catch you loafing and off your guard.

Day 16 - Don't Let The Enemy Catch You Loafing

Once while serving on jury duty, we heard the case of a young man who was killed because it was rumored that he was loafing. Like me, many of my co-jurors had no idea of the meaning of this slang word that the young people were using. The young man explained the term loafing meant you were "chillin," relaxing, being lazy, and not paying attention. Because the young man had made enemies, he was made aware that the enemy could be lurking around at any time to find an opportune time to strike. In the dangerous games that he played, he knew that he had to be on high alert at all times, watching, looking and cautious. There was not a time that he could lower the alert to low watch or even moderate watch. This particular day he decided that because everything was on the even kill, nothing had happened in a while, he thought that he was just going to hang out with his girlfriend and just "chill." Little did he know that the enemy was on high alert that day, looking, spying out the land, moving around to see who was hanging out by themselves, anyone that was defenseless and alone.

That's just like the enemy, when you are tired, don't feel like being bothered, just need a little "R & R," this is the time when he wants to come in and attack because he knows that you are not paying attention. There are days when we all have not felt like praying, interceding, reading our Word, or spending time with God. This is known as spiritual loafing. We say today, we are just going to rest and do nothing at all. Little do we know that when we have confessed these words, that we open the door and invite the enemy to stop by. We open ourselves up for attack because we are not expecting the enemy to hit us. Let it be known that it's these times when the enemy will hit us the hardest. He knows that our focus and our mindset are on vacation mode. We have logged off and he can get in the first punch 9 times out of 10 and do some major harm. That's why the Bible tells us in 1 Peter 5:8 "Be well balanced (temperate, sober of mind), be vigilant and cautious at all times; for that enemy of yours, the devil, roams around like a lion roaring [in fierce hunger], seeking someone to seize upon and devour." Because the enemy doesn't play fair and never has, we have to always be on our post. We can't afford to come down off the wall; we can't afford to take a vacation from reading the Word, praying, studying, or encouraging one another. <u>When the Bible tells us to pray without ceasing, that doesn't sound like there is any place to take a break to me</u>; that doesn't sound like doing it when you feel like it; that doesn't sound like every other day or once a week either. It's at the times when we don't want to, that we need to push the hardest. It's at these times when we want to rest and take a break, or have a lazy moment that we need to do it the most. We need to let our flesh know that it's not in charge and the enemy understands that he cannot persuade us to trade in our access privileges. One thing I have learned that when you make the sacrifice to do it because God has said to do it, the blessing, the reward, the access that is waiting is well worth it. It's these times, more often than not, that the Lord wants us to know it's not about us but about His will.

So when you feel like loafing, remember who you are inviting in and what may go along with when you pause from doing what God told you to do. Loafing doesn't live here anymore.

Reflections:
Please take this seriously, if you are loafing, the enemy will catch up to you? Do you really want that! I don't think so. So what are you doing to prevent this from happening?

Day 17 – There Is No Place Like Being In God's Presence

I'm reminded of the movie the *Wizard of Oz*. Dorothy wants badly to go home, so she stops at nothing to get there. She is given instructions to get there. "Follow the yellow brick road and that will lead you home." On her journey home, she is faced with many obstacles. Her biggest distraction is the wicked witch who stops at nothing to discourage, distract and delay her journey. When she finds out that the yellow brick road is not the answer, she is told very simply by the good witch of Oz that the way to get there is to believe. As she began to believe, she remembered and kept saying "There's no place like home."

Like Dorothy, Christians are faced with obstacles when they try to get into God's presence. <u>When we seek to get into God's presence, the enemy will stop at nothing to stop us</u>. He understands that there is no place like being in His presence. The Bible tells us that God is a rewarder to those who seek Him. When you press into His presence, the benefits are priceless. You will find joy, peace, love, rest, assurance and let's not forget hope.

Like Dorothy, when you have been in the presence of God, you will stop at nothing to return to it every chance you can. If you have never experienced it, I encourage you; seek God with your whole heart, mind and body. Let nothing stop you from being in His presence.

> Psalms 16:8 – "I have set the Lord always before me because He is at my right hand. I shall not be moved. Therefore my heart is glad and my glory rejoices my flesh will always rest in hope. For you will not leave my soul in Sheol. Nor will you allow your Holy One to see corruption. You will show me the path of life. In your presence is fullness of joy at your right hand are pleasures for evermore."

Reflections:
Lord teach me how to enter into your presence. When I'm in God's presence, I feel like:

Day 18 – Now What?

Have you ever gotten to the place that you say to God, "Now what? Where am I to go now?" All the avenues have been blocked or either closed. Everything that you thought should have happened, thought would have happened and even could happen has now seemed to faded, fizzled or just flown away.

It sort of reminds me of the children of Israel. They have now left Egypt; left the place that has kept them in bondage, the place where they could not grow, and could not reach their Promised Land. As Pharaoh allowed them to begin their journey, then comes something else. They thought that since Pharaoh had allowed them to leave Egypt that they were on easy street. Everything was supposed to be good, they could now breathe again. Life was going to be grand in the Promised Land, but then the Lord allowed Pharaoh to change his mind, hardened his heart and then realize what he had done was crazy. Sounds like anything that you're going through? You may be thinking, Now that I have said yes to God, I'm on my way to where He has called and made promises to me and here comes this? It was not supposed to happen like this? I was supposed to be able to move right into the place where the Lord showed me.

But just like God told the children of Israel, "Keep on moving and don't stop, looking back at what is happening now." It's only to put His glory on display and for all the naysayers to know without a shadow of a doubt that God was in this all along. Just as He wiped out Pharaoh's army, He will also do the same with your enemies. Not only did He do this but God also allowed them to see. He prepared a table before them in the presence of their enemies; He allowed them to watch as He took them out. Can I just encourage you, that some of your naysayers, after this one, you won't see again. They will learn that those who had a hand in trying to keep you down will think about it before they bother another one of God's anointed.

So now when I say "Now what?" I have a different way of saying it. Now What? The enemy can bring it on, but I know that God will bring me to victory.

Be encouraged....

Reflections:
God please show me what's next for me. What I see is not all that you have for me.

Day 19 - "Don't Count Me Out!"

Isn't it amazing how people can so easily be ready to count you out! They can just push out of their mouths, "You can't do this or you won't make it." They feel because the stacks against you seem so high that you will never make it! They look at your situation, they look at you, and all they see is defeat. All they see with their eyes is that this situation you are in may be too much for you to handle. Could it be that because they are looking with their own eyes and can picture themselves in this situation, that maybe they feel as if they couldn't handle it and that automatically puts you in the same category?

When they look at the situation, just the idea alone dictates that you shouldn't be here because you should have lost your mind, you should have gone "coo-coo for co-co puffs," you should have given up, you should have quit. You are still here, you're still standing. It should be a sign that you are stronger than they thought.

The odds may be against you, the situation may seem dim, disappointing and discouraging, but I've got to let you know you will make it! This is when God works best. You will get to where you got to go! You will come out of this one too! You needed this one to put in your testimony chest! You had to take this one for someone else! You were created for this one to be a blessing! Because this one had your name on it, God already knew that you were going to come out of this one!

Didn't God bring you through past struggles when you didn't think you would survive? So what makes you think it won't happen this time? It's only temporary! Get yourself up! Brush yourself off! The word of God says in 1 Corinthians 2:9: "Eye has not seen, nor ear heard, nor have entered into the heart of man the things which God has prepared for those who love Him."

Let me encourage you today! They may try to count you out! They may even think that you are down for the last count! They may say that you won't even make it! But just smile and know within your heart "You ain't seen nothing yet!" <u>Just wait until they see what comes out of this</u>!

Reflections:
Are you allowing people to count you out, put you down, and tell you that you can't make it? Today the buck stops here! Don't let anyone count you out!

Day 20 - It Ain't Over Yet!

When I think of the word "yet," it tells me that it has not happened at this particular time. "Yet" tells me that regardless of what is happening in the situation, something is about to change. While you're thinking that the particular situation that you may be facing is done, is over, and is finished. God said to add the word "yet" to let you know that He's not finished with this particular situation in your life. You may think that it's done and man may have said that it's over, that situation may have even presented itself as complete, but "It ain't over yet"—until God says "It's over."

This is the time that you need to declare:

I will not die but I shall live.
I'm not going to fear for God is with me.
In the time of trouble, He shall hide me.
I will wait on the Lord and be of good courage.

<u>Turn your problems into praise and your worries into worship</u>. Remind yourself the next time you are in a situation that you don't know what to do or how you're going to come out, "It ain't over yet." When you come through this, you will be better and you will be wiser; you will also be better equipped to handle the next thing that God allows. Thank Him that He has allowed you to pass through the storm, through the valley, not to kill you, but to make you stronger. Begin to thank God for strength to go through because "It ain't over yet."

Reflections:
It ain't over "until the fat lady sings" but when my God says that it's over!

Day 21 - "I Know It's Going To Be Alright."

Have you ever been along "Don't Know Street?" Don't know how you are going to make it? Don't know how you are going to see your way out of a particular situation? Don't know if your children will get through the situation they find themselves in? Don't know if the ends will meet? Don't know if you will find a job? Don't know if they will come and get your stuff today because you already know you will be evicted? Don't know how you will pass the test? You just "plain ole" don't know what's going to happen? Along "Don't Know Street" can oftentimes be long and lonely.

But I've got good news for you today! It's going to be alright.

I don't know how God is going to work it out. I don't know when He is going to work it out? I don't ever know who He will use to work it out. All I know and can hold on to is that He will work it out. I don't know if it will be today, tomorrow or next week but I know that He will work it out.

I come to encourage you today; I know it's a heavy load to bear; I know that it doesn't seem like it will ever end; situation after situation; and problem after problem stacking up against you, but all I know is that God is able. I can take a page from Daniel around the third chapter where we find the Hebrew boys in a fiery situation and they were able to declare that the God that they served was able.

So if it worked for them then I know that it can work for you today because He is the same God yesterday, today and forevermore. That's why you can say that God is able! And because you know that He is able you know that He will work it out! So when you find yourself on "Don't Know Street," keep on walking and know that it's going to be alright!

Reflections:
God help me to trust you more and more each day. If I have to say it every day, "Lord I trust you" to get it deep in my spirit then I'm willing to do just that.

Day 22 - Take Off Those Glasses

Have you ever been in a situation when you thought that it was done, it was final, it was a wrap and now you have come to the mourning stage? Whew! In fact your mind was on the way to the cemetery. Your mind had already had your family and friends over for hours. You were discussing the situations, what had happened. You were reminiscing on the good times, the bad times, things that made you laugh and remembering how it all took place. Now you are in a place in your mind where you are beginning to accept the fact that the situation is dead. You rehearsed so many times in your mind, God won't let this happen. You know what He has done before; You know how He got you out of the other ones and you do trust that He is always there. Somehow, you just can't let go of the fact of all that He has done for you. You know what He promised, you know what He had said, and you know who He is and what He can do. When you look through your glasses the signs of life were gone, nothing remained, lifeless, it was a flat-lined mess. As you were walking to its final destination, getting ready to accept the fact that it was over, you were saying your last good bye.... Here comes the Lord telling you to "Take off those glasses because what you have been seeing has all been in your imagination. You have allowed the glasses to cover truth. You couldn't see not only that I was there but that the situation was designed to make you turn back. The glasses were so deceptive that you were losing sight of the fact that all things are possible, even when they looked dead. <u>You were losing sight of the fact that I am God and I can do anything that I want to do</u>. You have lost sight to the fact that if I will a thing or make a promise to you, I have to perform it because My name is on the line. There are times when I need to allow the enemy to think that he is winning in your life just to prove to him that I am still God. You are mine and you will not turn back no matter what hits you, no matter what comes your way, and no matter what I take away. I just needed to use you as an example today so that My name is glorified in what appeared as though it would take you out of here."

So understand, nope, it wasn't a wrap, it wasn't done, it wasn't the final season nor show. So let me help you out, don't allow the glasses to stop you from where you need to focus or head. Don't allow the glasses to distort who I Am in your life. Don't allow the glasses to make you look in another direction other than Me. Allow Me to continue to be the Author and Finisher of your faith because in this season it is a faith walk. The ropes will get tight but you must believe with your mind and your heart that I AM who I have declared and shown you that I AM. I AM actually much more than that but I allow you to see Me differently at each level that you reach. So today, see Me as your Source and Resource and know that I will never steer you in the wrong direction because I love you.

Reflections:
Let me help you out on this one, the glasses will distort your vision! See for yourself.

Day 23 - I Sent The Holy Ghost To Break Up This Party

I know there have been times that you've wanted to throw up your hands and quit. If you're like me, you've said it once, you may have even said it a few times, God this is it. You don't want to hear another thing? You feel like throwing up your hands and saying, "Stick a fork in me, I'm done." What's worse is then "I Don't Care" decides to come to the party, too. <u>You begin to dance with "I Don't Care" and you really don't want to do anything... anymore.</u>

But just when you think that it's done, God will send the Holy Spirit to come in and break up the party. He does this by using other people to come to your rescue, sometimes getting on your nerve. They want to encourage you and tell you things like: "This is not you, you can make it, you are more than a conqueror, you are loved, it's time to get up from this place." All the things that you don't want to hear, here they come with it. Ask Jeremiah, when he was at his wits end, he is reminded that it is time to end the party. "This I recall to my mind therefore I have hope, it's because of your mercy that we are not consumed, great is thy faithfulness."Lamentations 3:23.

Aren't you glad that God is a Keeper? Even when we don't want to be bothered, we want to throw in the towel, God is faithful. Yes what you are feeling is real but God knows exactly what you need. That's why He takes precautions and sends the very best, the Holy Spirit. He is such a gentleman that He just won't barge in but when it's time for the party to be over, He sends someone. That's the kind of God we serve. So have your party if you must but know that God won't let the party last too long.

Reflections:
Aren't you glad that God knows what you need? He promised that He will never leave you nor forsake you so even when you are having a pity party, He comes there, too.

Day 24 - On The Wings Of Waiting

Have you ever been in the posture of waiting? You know what God has said and He has shown you a snippet of your dreams, desires, and destiny but He has not yet allowed you to reach that place. Why do you have to wait you ask? There is a place in waiting that brings out character, trust and belief in God. When we have to wait and can do it without complaining, without getting frustrated, we have gathered a gem. Waiting is not easy but when you learn how to wait on the Lord, you learn how to be of good courage. You learn that God will give you strength; you learn that something better comes when you wait on the Lord. You can wait patiently when you believe that which you will receive is on the way.

"Desperate and helpless and longing," I cried.
Patiently, lovingly my Lord replied.
I pled and I wept for a clue to my fate;
And the Master so gently said, "Child, you must wait."
"Wait? You said 'wait?'" my indignant reply.
"Lord, I need answers. I need to know why.
Is Your hand shortened or have You not heard?
By faith I have asked, and I'm claiming Your Word.
My future and all to which I can relate
Hangs in the balance, and You tell me wait.
I'm needing a yes, a go-ahead sign,
Or even a no to which I can resign.
And Lord, You promised that if we believe
We need but to ask and we shall receive.
And Lord, I've been asking, and this is my cry,
I'm weary of asking, I need a reply."
Then quietly, softly, I learned of my fate
As my Master replied once again, 'You must wait.'
So I slumped in my chair defeated and taught,
and grumbled to God, "So I'm waiting for what?"

A Dose of Encouragement

He seemed then to kneel, and His eyes wept with mine,
And He tenderly said, "I could give you a sign.
I could shake the heavens and darken the sun;
I could raise the dead, cause the mountains to run.
All you seek I could give, and pleased you would be.
You would have what you want, but you wouldn't know Me.
You'd not know the depths of My love for each saint;
You'd not know the power that I give to the faint.
You'd not learn to see through the clouds of despair;
You'd not learn to trust just by knowing I'm there.
You'd not know the joy of resting in Me
When darkness and silence were all you could see.
You'd never experience that fullness of love
As the peace of My Spirit descends like a dove.
You'd know that I give and I save, for a start,
But you'd not know the depth of the beat of My heart,
The glow of My comfort late in the night,
The faith that I give when you walk without sight,
The depth that's beyond getting just what you asked of an infinite God
Who makes what you have last.
And you'd never know, should your pain quickly free,
What it means that My grace is sufficient for thee.
Yes, your dreams for that loved one overnight may come true,
But oh the loss if I lost what I'm doing in you.
So be silent, my child, and in time you will see
That the greatest of gifts is to get to know Me.
And though oft may My answers seem terribly late,
My most precious of all is still, Wait."
Author Unknown

It may not be time yet but as my grandmother often said, He may not come when you want Him but He is always on time....

Reflections:
Lord if I can be honest with you I don't like to wait because:

Day 25 - There Is Power Behind What We Say……

Growing up in church, there are many clichés that we have learned. "God is good all the time." "If it had not been for the Lord on my side!" "God is a good God." "God is able." We say these words but do we really mean what we say? Its sounds good and we know when and where to insert them but are we really sincere when we say them?

Do we really know the power that's behind confessing these words? If we really knew the power that was behind words, we would trust God in everything. If we really knew the power that was behind these words, we would be able to speak life not only into our own situation but into someone else's as well. The Bible tells us in Proverbs 18:21, you have the power to speak life or death into your situation, but it's up to you.

The next time that you want to say something negative, think about what you are saying.

So take it from a wise proverb "When life hands you lemons, make lemonade."

Instead of saying "it won't" say "it will."

Instead of saying "it's impossible" say that "it is possible."

Instead of saying "I can't" say "I can do all things through Christ that gives me strength."

Instead of saying "my situation doesn't look good" say "God is able."

Instead of saying "my cup is half empty", say "my cup is half full."

Instead of saying "my life is in turmoil," thank God that you are still living. Instead of frowning, smile.

<u>Speak life, it's up to you</u>. You set your own atmosphere with what you

say. Life can be difficult, but you have the power to turn your situation around with positive confessions.

Reflections:
Do you need to watch what you say? Make a promise to yourself that the words that come out of your mouth will be positive.

Day 26 – Stop "Trippin"...

Have you ever been in a point in your life where you seem to have forgotten who God really is? Okay, for a slight moment maybe you were hit on the head and spiritual amnesia took over. A problem arises in your life and you say that you are okay, you let people think that you are fine but you begin to get a little weary. The enemy really begins to come at you with all kinds of stuff – "See I told you that you were not good enough;" "I told you that you were going to mess up again," "I told you that God would not allow this to happen."

It's happened too many times that we allow the enemy to creep in and steal our joy and our peace. We allow him to say what he will say and roll right on off the scene, leaving us in a weary state of being.

<u>When those times arise, you've got to take out the resume of your life and remember all that God has already brought you through</u>. Maybe you don't get it so let me come down your street. He brought me through the accident; He brought me through the abuse; and He brought me through homelessness; He brought me through bankruptcy; He brought me through a divorce; He brought me through unemployment; He brought me through the surgery and the list goes on and on. All that God has already done should be enough for us to know that He will bring us through this, too. Sometimes God has to raise our level of faith. Sometimes God has to see that no matter what occurs, we are still going to praise Him. How are we going to respond in this situation?

That's why one song writer said "Lord you've been so faithful." Another one said "I can truly say that I've been blessed and I've got a testimony." That which you have endured only adds to your resume and your testimony chest of how God brought you through. So stop "trippin," brush the dust off and keep it moving.... God's got this one, too!

Reflections:
I need to stop "trippin" off of the small stuff. If I say that God can do it then I need to believe it. Don't let it just be lip service but put it into action.

Day 27 - Your Thinking Is Too Small

Too many times we have this syndrome called T.T.S. - "Thinking Too Small." <u>Our expectation of what God can do is minimal</u>. We say that we believe but in reality we don't. If we really did, then when God does something that we have asked, it wouldn't be a surprise to us. We oftentimes act like we didn't think that He could actually do what we asked Him to do. We sit back, ask, and then don't believe. Or we only think that God can do little things, like pay our bills, or give us a car. These things are nothing to God. Your thinking is really too small, if all you expect God to do is to get you a house or buy you a car.

It's when we begin to ask God for things that we can't finance that stretches our faith. The funds needed to start your own business, or to write a book, or to start your ministry are things we may not be able to finance but God can. The Bible tells us that He can do exceeding, abundantly, above all that you can imagine. What about the things that you have dreamed about? The things that God has promised you that you just can't believe that you can have. If God has said it, then your level of expectation has to grow. A lot of times, God will put this in your spirit just to see what you will do. Can God? God can if you believe it. Can you? It was never meant for you to be able to, it was meant for God. That's the problem, we look at our abilities, we look at our finances and we say we can't afford to do something at this particular time in our lives. So we take a page from Sarai's and sit back and laugh. We say "Really God; you want to do what in my life. This thing that I had in my mind, the thing that you promised years ago? Are you kidding! If it were going to happen, it would have already happened? If you were going to do this, you would have already done it." God is saying to you, "It can still happen. Just because you put a time limit on Me, I purposefully didn't allow it to happen so that when your enemies had their last laugh, I would show up and you would have no problem identifying that this was Me who did it."

So stop thinking small. Supersize your faith! It's not always easy but take small steps. When God begins to blow your mind, you will raise your level of expectation. What's the worst that can happen? That it doesn't happen. But what if it does happen….

Change your thinking. Take the limits off God.

Reflections:
Dream today! What things do you want and can't afford? Now thank God for them and raise your level of expectancy of what God can do.

Day 28 – Stay In Your Lane

Times are not like they use to be and that can be a good thing. However, in today's society, we see something that we like that someone else has. If it looks good on them, then you imagine that it will look good on you, too. If you see them prospering, you want to try and do the same thing that they did to get where they are today.

When we want what someone else has or try to be like someone else, we find ourselves somewhere that was never designed for us. We find ourselves in what I call "Someone Else's Lane." What is designed for someone else, you have no right to walk in it. You are out of order, out of place, out of control and God cannot bless where you are. It's as if people will look at you and look at an assignment that needs to be completed or even a title that needs a name attached to it and you quickly sign up for it with little thought about it. Yes you may have the skills, the abilities, the "I can always get the job done attitude," but that's not really the lane that has been designed just for you. If we are not careful, we will find ourselves doing a good thing but in reality it's not a God thing.

Let me help you, you need to stay in your lane. It's only when you stay in your lane that you can have all that God has for you. <u>Don't get in a head-on collision, being out of place</u>. Don't end up somewhere else. Get out of someone else's lane so that they can do what they have been called to do. You are holding them up and holding yourself back all because you won't stay in your lane. It's time to move and get back in your lane. If you don't know what your lane is, seek God and ask Him what it is that He has designed just for you. You might be surprised to discover what God has in store for you.

Reflections:
Can you honestly admit that you are in the wrong lane... just doing something because it needs to be done? Can you honestly say that is what God has for you?

Day 29 - Everybody Can't Go

If you're anything like me, you think that you can save the world and help everybody. If someone is in need, you go and try to help in any way that you can. I have learned a valuable lesson and know that you can't help everybody and everybody can't go where you go. People will try to use you and suck the very life out of you, if you are not careful.

On your journey in life, people will come in and out of your life. God will allow them in your life for a season and then it's meant for them to be gone. He will allow you to get what you need from them and then it's meant for them to exit. It's nothing personal, it's not that they don't want to be bothered but their assignment in your life is over. Many times we want to keep holding on to them. They may have made a great impact in your life, and you have deemed them to be true friends. They may have spoken numerous words of encouragement and prophecies over you, but when their time is up, you must let them go. God may not have ever intended for them to go in the first place, but you had to go and think you couldn't do without them. <u>Jesus never took the entire twelve disciples; most of the time, He only took three</u>. When Abraham was going to sacrifice his son, Isaac, he told his servant to wait at a certain spot. On your journey, there will be some that will stay and those who will not. Just know that God knows who needs to be with you and who doesn't. There will be a period in your life when God intends for you to be alone so that He can get some things accomplished in your life. If you have some people around you, they may distract or hinder you. Love them while they are in your life but know and accept when the time has come for them to go. Embrace the truth that everybody can't go where God is taking you.

Reflections:
Are there people that you want to take with you to your next level in the Lord but you know that you cannot take them? It's a hard decision to not include them. If they care about your walk with the Lord, they will understand and only want what's best for you. Pray and ask God for direction.

Day 30 – Help Me, I'm Being Held Hostage By Unforgiveness

Unforgiveness is a spiritual disease that has crippled many people in our society. This "disease" call unforgiveness strikes everyone, no matter if you are black or white, rich or poor, Christian or non-Christian, young or old, live on the north side or west side, it affects us all. Unforgiveness does not have any particular person's name on it because at one time or another, we have all allowed this disease to rent a room in our temple. What's even more sad is that many people leave this earth not choosing to forgive someone who has wronged them.

Unforgiveness is when we allow someone else to have control over our emotions. We are incapable of releasing them for what they have done. It cripples us so much that we are not able to move forward. I have witnessed how it has stopped people from reaching their possibilities, potential, and purpose. Unforgiveness is detrimental to your health. Those who harbor it open the door to so many other spirits. I discovered that unforgiveness holds us hostage and when we want to let it go, it finds friends for us to play with like anger, hostility, hatred, misery, and bitterness. When their friends come along, they don't play fair because they will then bring their other friends. The next thing you know, you find yourself emotionally drained, physically damaged and spiritually despondent.

Can I just encourage you today, let it go? Don't give power to this thing call unforgiveness. I can honestly agree with you when you say that it hurts. Someone did you wrong or you never thought they would do to you what was done. Yes I know that they really messed you up, broke your heart, left you wounded but I come today to invite you to a place in God called freedom. <u>Don't be a part of the silent statistics and allow unforgiveness to kill you.</u> Today, choose to honestly forgive. Don't let unforgiveness hold you hostage by saying "I'll forgive you but I won't forget what you did." If you allow this to happen, every time that you see the person, it will bring up the anger and bitterness in your heart and to be honest with you, you still haven't forgiven them. Forgiving someone is not for them, but for you. You are releasing yourself so that you can move forward. Don't let unforgiveness hold you hostage.

Reflections:
Today, I am honestly going to let it go. I am forgiving:

Day 31 – I'm Finally Walking Out Of This Prison

The National Negro College Fund commercial would come on the TV at the most opportune times. It was known for its slogan "A Mind Is A Terrible Thing To Waste." I would think about that and ponder why they would say that. But when I came into the revelation that the mind is the central location for things to happen in our bodies, I could understand why. It's in the mind that everything is processed and then released to tell our bodies what to do. I have often heard the older saints in church say that an idle mind is the devil's workshop. <u>If we are not keeping our minds in order, focused, determined to do the right thing, the enemy will use it as a playing field to play all kinds of tricks</u>. He will try and use our minds to get us to go against everything that God has promised in the Word. If he can get you out on the field by entertaining these thoughts, he knows that you will play with him. That's why we have to be so careful to keep our minds on Jesus. We have to cast down any imagination that tries to exalt itself against the knowledge of God and bring it into captivity by letting our flesh know that it has to come under the authority of Christ.

For so long, we have allowed the enemy to keep us held in bondage in our minds. If your mind is locked up, all tied up, confused, or messed up, you don't want to hear or receive truth. You think that the way you are is okay. You want to be left alone, don't want to hear another Scripture, another sermon, or hear nothing about what is right. You can't see clearly because your vision has taken a vacation and your ministry is missing in action. You catch every bus that comes up and down your street and other wrong doctrines. Obedience is not even on the agenda.

Can I just share with you that there was a time when I wasn't free? There was a time where the enemy had my mind so twisted that the prison doors were open, but I couldn't find myself able to leave. However, when truth was made clear, it was time to give the enemy an eviction notice and walk off the prison grounds that were holding my mind. I am a living testimony that you can be set free. Today the prison that you've been locked up in opens. Free yourself, free your mind, free your spirit, as the Bible tells us in John 8:36 "Whom the Son has set free is free indeed." So are you free today? Are you able to allow your mind to be released because the chains had already been taken off by the Holy Ghost? It's time for you to walk out of the prison that is holding your joy, peace, rest, and your love. When you are ready to be free, you will allow truth, the doors will open, your faith can grow and God will restore you.

Reflections:
Today, I decree and declare that your mind is set free now! The doors are open, so get to walking!

Day 32 – Passing The Test Of Obedience

If you are like me, I don't like to take tests. Some people do well when they take them, typically because they have taken the time to study. For others, they will wait until the last minute to try and cram and the results are not always positive. Research has proven that 9 times out of 10, those who take the time to study will pass the test. Those who decide not to study or wait until the last minute usually fail or just barely pass.

I can tell you from experience that there will be times that God will test you to see if you are willing to do what He has requested. Not that God does not already know the results of the test, but it's mostly to let you know the status of your walk with Him. The Lord has said that most of us do not pass the test because we do not know His voice. In our minds we question, is this really you God? Because we are unsure of His voice, we have what I call "God show me a sign syndrome." God is saying that there will come a time when I will not show you another sign. You will either know that it's Me or stay stuck on uncertainty until you decide that you are sure that it's Me.

Because we receive low marks on the test of obedience and did not do what God told us, how can He allow us to get what He has for us? Most of us are stuck in the middle of hearing, but we're not moving. This has allowed the enemy to rob us of our time. Then, we have the audacity to say that we are waiting to hear from God; when in fact God is waiting on us to be obedient and move. He has such a great blessing but we cannot receive it until we have surrendered to His will. When we are obedient and do what He says, it will unlock the door to our blessing of, not just enough but, overflow. In Luke 5, God told Simon to let down his net and although he had been fishing all night and caught nothing, Simon said "Nevertheless because You have said it I will obey." Because of his obedience, God allowed an overflow to occur. Some of us have missed the same abundance that God has for us because we just won't obey. <u>It's our obedience that drives God to move</u>.

So as I take a page from Simon's book, move past the fear of the unknown, and surrender to do what God has said for you to do. There is so much that God has for you. Your overflow is waiting but you won't receive it until you have done what God has told you to do. Don't let the enemy rob you of your blessing because you didn't pass the test.

Reflections:
Are you being totally or partially obedient? What's holding you back from total obedience to the voice of God?

Day 33 - If It Ain't Broke Don't Fix It

Back in the day, there was a song that came out that said "...if it ain't broke don't fix it just relax and let it go," and I declare that there are people who are still living along these same lines. The problem that I have and that I believe we face is the fact that when things are broken we still don't want to get them fixed. If I can just be honest for a moment and let you know that there are some people who don't even know that there are some things which are broken. There are things in our lives that are broken of which we are not even aware. I know for myself that I had broken my toe but I didn't realize it. I knew that it felt a little different but I just thought that I hit it and that the pain was normal for a few days. The days turned into weeks and finally I decided to go to get it checked out and found out that it was broken. Well just like I didn't realize that it was broken, many times we don't know that our relationship with God has been broken, severed or even cut off. We go around as if everything is okay. In fact there are signs that are telling us but we tend to just ignore them. If we don't check, and our relationship grows farther and farther apart, and the next thing we know is that we are okay without being with God. Your mind begins to grow farther and farther away from wanting to be with Him. Then you begin to replace Him with something and someone else. Other things begin to take up all your time and the next thing you know, the grass looks greener on the other side and you are gone. <u>You have just been bamboozled, deceived and tricked by the enemy</u>.

But I've got good news for you, in these days we cannot afford to not have a relationship with God. We cannot afford to just go around with our ties severed or disconnected. We have to find a way to come back to the Father, because if today was like yesterday and an earthquake hit again, but this time Jesus returned, where would you spend your eternity? Can you honestly say that you will spend your eternity with God, and then when you meet with Him face to face, what will He say? Will He say, "Enter, you have been faithful over a few things." Or will

He say, "Depart from Me; I never knew you?" Will you cry Lord, I did all these things in your Name? Why can't I enter? And when He tells you with sorrow, "I never knew you, I never had a relationship with you; you never decided that you wanted me; you only called when there was trouble in your life, you thought that our relationship was okay but I beckoned to you. I called you and I sent others but you didn't have time for me." Don't let the Lord tell you this. Today, it's time to get your relationship with God in order while you still have time. Who knows, the next earthquake could be the very one that takes us out and will you be ready?

Reflections:
Do you know whether your relationship with God has been severed or disconnected? If you don't know, now is the time to check it.

Day 34 – Caller Are You There?

Have you ever felt God was asking you "Caller Are You There?" There was a time on your life's journey that you called Him; you couldn't wait to talk with Him; you read your Word every day and sometimes twice a day; you kept the radio and television channels on the gospel or Christian stations; or you would just bask in God's presence for hours. Then all of a sudden you got a new job, you got in a new relationship, you got a new house, you got a new car, started a gym membership, you started attending a new church or met a new friend and all of a sudden, God is saying "Caller Are You There?" Everyday-time spent with God went out the window. It went from every day, sometimes twice a day, to every 2 or 3 days in your time with God. Now it's once a week or every other week. You went from getting up early, to getting up five minutes before having to shower, eat and run to catch the train. You went from hours to one-half hour to minutes. God knows my heart. God knows that I need to have a life too. God knows that I'm human. He'll understand. "Caller Are You There?" He keeps asking of you. Have you gone back? Is what you are going through too much? "Caller Are You There?" "Oh God," you reply, "Here I am! You know today, I wasn't feeling too good." So days go by. "Caller Are You There?" "Yeah God, I'm here. I was just helping at the church, got busy doing things to help out." "Caller Are You There? I really miss you!" "Yes Lord, I'm here. I was hanging out last night, couldn't get up this morning." "Caller Are You There?" "Lord, I had to take care of the children; I had to take care of the pastor; I had to do school work; I had to spend time with me." "Caller Are You There? I guess you don't have time for me, so I won't hang up but I will just put you on hold!" So you do you.... "God, uh this is me. Today they gave me a pink slip, what am I going to do? God, my children have lost their minds for real. God are you there! God, the car broke down twice this week, God are you there! The people at church don't understand! God, do you hear me! God where are you? This is no joking matter, I really need you. God I once had access to you. At one time I could call on you and I knew that you heard me. I could once get in Your presence and know that everything was okay. God, hello.... God, God, God, God are You there? Lord, I'm so sorry for what I have done. I decided to do things on my own. I had access and now I know the meaning of losing my access and that's not a good feeling. So Lord, today I repent. I know that I have taken you for granted and I want my access back. I know that I will have to get back in right relationship with you. I'm sorry. <u>Lord, if you just would let me know that you hear me</u>. I know that you are a forgiving and loving God. Lord please restore me back to you because it was me that hung up the phone. God is that you." "Caller, Are You There?" "Yes Lord...."

Reflections:
Don't let God have to ask "Caller Are You There?" If He does, today is the time for true repentance.

Day 35 – Celebrate Your "Elevators"

We all have witnessed celebrities when they receive their Grammy, Academy, Oscar, BET or any other prestigious awards; they like to thank all the people who have helped them to get where they are. They thank their promoters, fans, agents, friends, families and some even take the time to thank God. But the ones I want to celebrate today are those who didn't wish me well; those who talked behind my back; even those who started out with me. They said that they would always be there for me but when the journey did not go the way that we all thought it would, they left me, forgot about me and forsakened me. Those who said it wasn't going to happen – all of these I want to classify as my "elevators."

So today, as I stand before you all I would like to give my speech for accepting my prestigious award!

Today I would like to celebrate my elevators. They helped to make me even more determined to keep on going simply because they didn't think that I could. Thank you for saying I would not arrive. Thank you for saying that this was too big for me to handle. Thank you for second guessing and doubting that God called me. Thank you for not believing me when I said that God had said it and you said He didn't. Thank you because you helped me to trust God like never before. Thank you because it was you that let me know I was right where God wanted me to be. It's partially because of you God allowed what you did to me to build my character, strengthen me for my journey, and push me into my destiny. You proved God's Word to be true that He would prepare a table before me in the presence of my enemies. God will "show you off" right in front of their faces. God will promote you and say "How you like Me now?," as He gets all the glory. It was you who helped me to stay in prayer, get closer to the Lord and learn to lean on Him in everything that I now do. You see I learned the real meaning in when God's Word says to pray for those who despitefully misuse you and say all manner of evil against you and who plot and set traps for you. Thank You! I celebrate you today that you have made my eyes and ears more sensitive to hear what God is saying and doing so that I can discern those wanting to do me harm. I thank you for tears that I shed because I was hurt, teaching me so many life lessons in what to do and not do. It taught me patience, but the most important lesson learned was how to show love in spite of how I was treated. It wasn't until I could forgive, heal, love and pray for my enemies that I could see the great work that God had done in me. So today I take the time to celebrate my "elevators." I understand that it was all a part of God's plan to use them, and they thought that they were using me. Now God gets all the glory from my life!

Reflections:
Take the time to pray for those who have hurt, mistreated or used you. It's only when you can pray for them and forgive them that you can celebrate what you have been through.

Day 36 - There's Something Great In You And It's Time That You Stir It Up

I easily encourage other people to do what they are called to do, but when it comes to me, it seems to be a difficult thing to do.

I Peter 4:10 tells us that God has placed gifts in each of us and Romans 12:6 also lets us know that He expects us to exercise what He has given to us. Some of us have allowed the enemy to convince us that we don't need to use our gift and just let it lie dormant. Some of us only want to do what we want; using our gift is not in the picture. Some people have not identified their gift and end up wasting time doing things that are outside of their gifting. Some people spin their wheels never knowing what's there or how to find out. They just hope and pray that it will go away. <u>What's in you is so great that God tailor made it just for you</u>. It gives the enemy great joy when we are unaware of our gifts. If they stay unidentified, we will not know how to use them to build up God's Kingdom and tear the enemy's down. It's when you know what your gift is that you become empowered and extremely dangerous. When you know what's in you, you know how to call on the name of Jesus, you know how to fight the enemy, and you know how to seek God. As long as the enemy keeps you in the dark, you can't do what you were suppose to do.

Not only do you need to be aware of your gift but you also need to know how to use it. It's not meant to be put up on a shelf, thrown away or forgotten. The gift that God has placed inside of you is for God's glory. Your gift is not for you but to bless others. It's meant to minister to those whom God places in your path. So what are you waiting for? It's time to get in gear, activate and stir up the gift that God has given to you. Don't let the enemy trick you and make you think that you don't have a gift or that you don't need it. Use it, stir it up, and activate it so that God will get the glory. It's in you! Stir it up!

Reflections:
To each of us God has given gifts. If you are unsure of what gift you have, it's time to find out. Seek God for direction and ask Him. Your gift is a gift to the Body of Christ.

Day 37 - You Were Not Called To Do Pigeon Ministry

"Why are you down hanging with the pigeons? Don't you know who you are? Don't you know whose you are? You are more anointed than that? So as I asked Adam, where are you, I'm asking YOU, where are you? Oh, there you are but why are you there? You are supposed to be up here! Eating up here not down there! How did you get back there! Who told you it was okay for you to be there! Do you know that your next level is way up here and not down there? Can you please tell Me what happened to the thermostat? I thought that we checked it on yesterday! I thought that it was already set!"

"Just as I asked Elijah the prophet when he ran from Jezebel, I'm asking you, why are you running? You should be running toward your enemy, your situation, not away from him or it! Your problem, like Elijah's, was that you got caught up in seeing your situation and not on the One who can show you, who is the Light for your path. Have you not seen what I have already done in your life, done to your enemies for you and on your behalf? So why are you here again? I never called you to Pigeon Ministry. Is it because your flesh keeps taking you back to that same place? No more excuses! As of today, that place will not be there the next time you go back. In this season if you try to run back you will miss Me while you are running back! You can't afford that this time. This season will be to come up higher in your prayer time, higher in your time with Me, higher in your relationship with Me, higher in your faith in Me."

"So when I call for you, when I ask you the next time, you will be where I can find you, not hanging below the radar and doing Pigeon Ministry. You will come up higher for as I have said before, I got you in this season. You've got to get to the next level, the next appointed place in Me. I will not come down while you want to do Pigeon Ministry, you must come up higher where I am. You will be able to be detected on My radar. Too low, no more, never again. Pick your spirit up and get to moving. The next step is waiting for you! How badly do you want to grow in Me?

How badly do you want what I have for you? Today, I command you to release the Pigeon Ministry because you can lose your life and miss Me! Let it go because Pigeon Ministry is not for you!"

Reflection:
This was a hard pill for me to swallow but it was the truth! Ouch...

Day 38 – You Messed With The Wrong One This Time!

Do I have a witness out there that is sick and tired of the devil? He hates me and I surely hate him. He tries and tries and tries and sometimes it seems like he doesn't know anybody else out here but me. I know that I have a target on my back, and he would love it if I bow out gracefully and give up on God. It would give him great pleasure if I would stop praying, stop preaching, stop loving, stop encouraging, stop ministering, just stop everything that God has called me to do. But boy didn't he make a mistake when he did not take me out when I was down and out. When I didn't think that I could make it. When I didn't think that I was good enough. When he didn't think that I would go on. But the God that's in me would not let me give up nor give in. <u>The God in me would not just let me lie down and die</u>. The God in me would not let me take my life. The God in me would not just give up on me. He empowered me, even the more, to let me know that there is some fight still left in me. It's time for you to learn how to fight the enemy. No, you are not fighting a physical fight but it's a spiritual one. You are not wrestling with flesh and blood but with principalities, with things that you can't see in the natural. So I have to teach you how to fight in the spirit.

God has shown me that when the enemy thinks that he has gotten you, then you get on your knees and pray. Pray that God will help you during this time. Pray that God will show you how to pray. Pray that God will equip you with what you need in order to fight the enemy. Get yourself in the posture of praise. Praise God in the middle of your storm. Praise God while you are going through and let the devil know that he has messed with the wrong one this time. Devil, "I know how to fight you. I know who I am and whose I am. And because I know who I am, when I am in a spiritual fight, I can go to my Father. He is my Strong Tower, He is my Protector, He is my Refuge and my Strength, He is my Shield and my Buckler, my God, and in Him will I trust. Devil I just want to put you on notice that you have messed with the wrong one this time. I know that you know my name and I surely know yours, too, but Greater is He that is in me than you."

Reflections:
Have you gotten fed up with the enemy messing with you? Well he is only doing his job. But you have to be on your post and ready when he comes. He comes for a season, but if you can just learn to rest in Jesus, everything will be alright.

Day 39 - "There Is Power In Your Praise!"

Did you realize that everything that you need is tied up in your praise? Praise says to God, thank you for what you have done! Praise tells God, I appreciate you! Praise says God I trust you! Praise elevates us to His presence and His power. The Bible tells us that God inhabits the praises of His people; He will come in their midst when He hears His children praising Him.

<u>Praise discharges strength in faith and a vehicle of faith which brings us into the presence and power of God and causes God to move on our behalf</u>. Ask King Jehoshaphat and his army in 2 Chronicles. When they began to praise the Lord, it set the hand of God in motion to defeat the enemy, even when the situation was unfavorable.

Praise can be the difference between victory and defeat. Praise can mean the difference between us coming out or staying just a little while longer. Praise can mean the difference between losing your mind and staying in perfect peace. Praise can mean the difference between fighting or standing still and trusting God to do it. Praise is our weapon that we have against the enemy; it's our garment that we can put on in battle. It's in your praise!

David said in Psalms 34: "I will bless the Lord at all times. When I feel like it and when I don't. No matter what I am going through, no matter what situation I find myself in, His praise shall continually be in my mouth...." It's in your praise....

Reflections:
Instead of worry, pouting, and complaining, I'm going to praise God for:

Day 40 – Unstoppable

The enemy will stop at nothing to hinder you from doing what you are supposed to be doing. One of his many jobs is to steal from you. If the enemy can steal your dreams, steal your time or even steal your focus, then he has succeeded. A lot of time, it's not really hard for the enemy to do this. Because nothing is new under the sun, he uses the same tactics that he has used before. He sits back in the cut and watches what ticks you off, what frustrates you, what angers you and then begin to use the same things against you. That's why when Staples came out with the "Easy" button, I wondered why in the world would they use such a concept. I believe that sometimes we make things easier for the enemy to trip us up than it should be. Sometimes we need to fool the enemy and do things a little different. The Bible says that if you resist him, he will leave you alone for a little while. Don't think because he didn't trip you up this time or got you to fall this time that he's not coming back. When the enemy gets ready to push the "Easy" button he ought to get back the reply "not this time." You ought to make up in your mind that he won't get me with this one. He may come with something I haven't dealt with but not this time. When he pushes the "Easy" button this time he will turn back scratching his head, what happened? I used to be able to get her with this and I use to be able to trip her with that. What has happened to her? Who has gotten to her and told her that she is more than a conqueror? Who told her that she can do all things through Christ Jesus, who gives her strength? Who told her that there is someone on the inside that is greater? Who told her that troubles don't last always? Who told her that if she trust in the Lord, surely He will make a way?

Today you need to put the enemy on notice; you can try and push the "Easy" button, but know that this time, it won't be easy with me. This time I've made up in my mind that I am unstoppable. You can do what you want to do; you can try what you want to try but this time, I've purposed in my heart that I am going to let nothing stop me from doing what I am called to do. <u>Destiny, watch out because here I come. Purpose, get ready because I'm on my way</u>. As the Word of God says in 1 Corinthians 15:58 "To stand firm and steady, immovable, firm, steadfast, not able to be shaken, keep on working for the Lord because in the end, what you do for the Lord you will not be able to say what was the point."

Reflections:
What are you allowing to stop you? Pray and ask God to help you to stay focused.

About The Author

Minister Sarah Branch was born and raised in Washington, D.C. to William and Barbara Branch. She was educated in D.C. Public School and received her Masters of Arts Degree in Biblical Studies from Maple Springs Baptist Bible College and Seminary in Capitol Heights, Maryland. She was licensed to preach in June 2001 at Third Baptist Church, Washington, DC. Minister Branch has ministered throughout the USA and Canada. She has a deep and profound appreciation of God for who He is and what He is capable of doing. She also treasures the anointing on her life and what she is called to do. In 2004, God birthed the ministry Destined For Victory designed to empower those to move in victory toward their God-given destiny. She has recently been given the Kingdom assignment to launch the Destined Diva's Conference Line, a ministry for teens and young ladies, to assist them in dealing with daily, real life issues. This line is open every Friday night at 9:00 pm. Minister Branch looks forward to Volume II of A Dose of Encouragement and has a high expectation for what God will do next. She enjoys her time with her three children, Jasmine, Donté and Ebony.

www.ingramcontent.com/pod-product-compliance
Lightning Source LLC
Chambersburg PA
CBHW071839290426
44109CB00017B/1874